4/92

Looking for .
in New Υ

I0634140

Looking for Angels
in New York

Poems by

Jacqueline Osherow

The University of Georgia Press

Athens and London

© 1988 by Jacqueline Osherow
Published by the University of Georgia Press
Athens, Georgia 30602
All rights reserved
Designed by Betty P. McDaniel
Set in Linotron Galliard
The paper in this book meets the guidelines for
permanence and durability of the Committee on
Production Guidelines for Book Longevity of the
Council on Library Resources.

Printed in the United States of America

92   91   90   89   88   5   4   3   2   1

Library of Congress Cataloging in Publication Data
Osherow, Jacqueline.
Looking for angels in New York.

I. Title.
PS3565.S545L66   1988   811'.54   88-4797
ISBN 0-8203-1059-X (alk. paper)
ISBN 0-8203-1060-3 (pbk. : alk. paper)

British Library Cataloging in Publication Data available

for my parents

The publication of this book is supported by a grant
from the National Endowment for the Arts,
a federal agency.

Acknowledgments

The author and publisher gratefully acknowledge the following publications where several of these poems first appeared.

Denver Quarterly: "South for Winter"
The Georgia Review: "The Presence of the Lute"
The New Yorker: "Looking for Angels in New York"
Shenandoah: "International Call," "To an Unknown Russian Poet"
Tikkun: "The Yiddish Muses"
Times Literary Supplement: "A Poem About Angels"

The author has many people to whom she owes thanks—for taking an interest in her work, encouraging it, taking her to the places that have inspired it, and inspiring it themselves. She believes they know who they are and hopes they are aware of her immense gratitude. She is particularly grateful to Jeff Rubin, who in one way or another has had an effect on almost every one of these poems, and Saul Korewa, who makes everything possible.

Contents

Five

One

Nostalghia

in memory of Andrei Tarkovsky,
April 4, 1932–December 29, 1986

At the end of the movie, snow falls
Into the roofless church of San Galgano
And the dead hero's exile dissolves.
We see a Russian landscape through the ruined
Colonnades of the cathedral, their
Shadowy, gray-gold Roman travertine
Blurred by Russian snow, that floats like stray
White feathers. It is as if a flock of geese
Has shed its wings above a liquid globe.

I have forgotten that the hero's dead,
What theater I am in, what city, I'm
Staring at the church, the birches, places
I have never been, and know this new place,
Where they meet, by heart. It is a picture
I have tried to see so many times,
Dreamed, if dreams can be invisible,
If it is possible to dream a picture
That you cannot see. I wanted all
The places I have loved in one picture,
The places I have missed where I have been,
Like this man's birches and his frozen pond
In his Italian Romanesque cathedral,
All pieces of a giant paperweight
I'm sitting in, a souvenir of dreams
Shaken upside-down to fill with snow.

You can't know what, in New York, this means
To me, three months back from Italy.
(It is New York when I get out, Lincoln

Center's geysers saving water, crowds,
Articulate, unmoved, clogging Broadway
With discussions of the film. I walk
Down streets I know but cannot recognize,
Filled with stores I cannot place, selling
Things I didn't know that people own.)
I lived in the Italy the Russian shows
Where angels, one with green, one, purple, wings,
Draw curtains on a pregnant Madonna
On a wall to which you've brought, willingly or not,
An incompatible, expansive landscape.

My Italian friends do not believe
That skyscrapers have separate elevator
Banks for groups of floors, that you go down
To get from twenty-three to forty-four,
Change cars in the lobby and go up.
We watch the Russian movie on RAI Uno.
Snowflakes float like feathers over stone.
When it ends, we leave the television on
And listen to the panel discussion.
In the kitchen making coffee, I can hear
An old woman, the Contessa Tolstoy,
Speaking slightly weighted-down Italian.
She must explain the title's meaning, *Nostalghia*.
Her tongue relaxes on the Russian word.

It is not your Italian nostalgia.
It is not longing for your distant home.
It is not dreaming of my father's house
From my house in Florence, but sleeping
In my father's house after sixty years
To dream of sleeping in this house when I was young.

I strain to see the old contessa's dream,
How, first, she sees the bed itself, of feathers,

The pillowcase and sheets embroidered snow,
And then the sounds begin, almost inaudible,
Of housemaids readying the others' beds,
Filling flannel-covered bottles with hot water.
Downstairs, there is a light beneath the door
Where she has never been allowed to enter.
Behind it, while she's sleeping, Moscow burns.

In her bed at Yasnia Polnaya,
The young girl in the dream begins to dream.
The woman she has chosen to become
Is handed down from carriages in cities
She has molded out of smooth, French names
A wistful, aging governess has taught her:
Paris, Vienne, Genève, Venise, Florence.
(*Florence.* The word must wake her. Sixty years
To learn that, after all, she's lived a dream.)
She thinks it is a place in southern France
Quite near to the small town in the Vaucluse
Where Mademoiselle once lay in bed and lulled
Herself to sleep, whispering, "*Moscou, Moscou.*"

Is this why we trade our dreams for *nostalghia?*
We cannot bear the stinging counterproofs,
The cities as they really are, blurs
Behind the details of our daily bouts
With disappointment, obstacles to work
That must get done. Perhaps it is our old,
Untarnished selves that we are looking for,
Selves that could concentrate, complete a dream,

Who never would have walked, as we have walked,
Past frescoed churches without entering
To move among the floating walls of saints,
Or driven countless times the quickest route
From Florence to Grosseto, unaware

How close they came to seeing San Galgano.
I have been there since I saw the film.
Dry, gold meadows filled the open-air
Cathedral and swallows perched in petals
Of the hollowed-out rose window and
Flitted among capitals and arches,
Their dark-gray feathers drifting on the stones.
I missed the haunted Russian man, the snow.

I should have gone to my old house and dreamed.
Home, there's little hope of *nostalghia*.
New York is not an easy place to dream.
There is always too much interference
From the movie theaters, from the dreamers
Dreaming down the hall, downstairs, upstairs,
In other buildings. All the visions meant
For us just crowd into a sky already
Crowded with a million unclaimed dreams
That hang, invisible, above our heads
Like the images that Einstein theorized
Repeat in air the pieces of our lives
And wait for us to pass the speed of light.

I know with *nostalghia* we could pass it
And gather up the floating images
To reunite the real-life shots with dreams.
I would try to fuse the pairs together,
Back to back, and with my handwork make
A private, retroactive tarot deck,
One side of each card a moment lived,
And on the other side, the moment's pulse,
Its buried, visionary hiding place,
The dream within the *nostalghia* dream.

Would it be bearable to flip the cards?
To read a future I've already missed

Until the real-life pictures reappear
As dreams, as if it was the past I longed for
When I longed to see the dreams behind
The pictures, *nostalghia,* the very dreams
I have no courage to see. The hero drives
For miles to see the pregnant Madonna,
The angels with the green or purple wings.
Then, when he arrives, he does not enter.
Does he prefer to stand outside and dream,
Or is it that he does not dare to come
Face to face with his own paltriness?

Instead, Tarkovsky makes us face our own.
He puts the great Madonna on the screen
And follows her with vision after vision:
Worlds in drops of rain on floors of shacks
With leaky roofs, birches, madmen, doves,
This brutal miracle of *nostalghia*
Emptying the sky of our lost footage,
Our pictures falling on the falling snow
That fills the roofless church of San Galgano
Where the hero has irrevocably gone
And everything we've ever known or seen
Vanishes for us to take this in.

Sonnet

after Lorenzetti's Deposition from the Cross

He is like a cloud that for an instant
Shaped a man, but has begun to spread,
To stretch the limbs, the torso, twist the head
So that it falls, upside-down, against
His mother's, her forehead to his cheek,
Her eye against his closed eye. And his thick
Gold hair filters through her hands like sand.
One saint bends to kiss a foot, one a hand,
One holds him just beneath the falling arm
And one more holds the thighs, presses his lips
Against the cloth that covers them and weeps.
What is the Resurrection to them?
It will not stay those thighs, those arms, that hair,
This thin, white mist that soon will disappear.

Fifth Stop on a Day Trip:
Trevi, Umbria

after Perugino's Adoration of the Magi

A gentle rustling along the wall
As Mary, Joseph, and the Magi move
Back in position and the thick crowds still.
I can't shake the feeling they've been dancing.
It's their litheness, their tilted heads, their robes.
And behind them, opening, a landscape—
Green to blue, plains to hills, clear skies to haze—
Seems to be moving still, to spread until I'm sure
It contains all Umbria: white-pink stone towns,
Olive-dotted hills, fortresses that float
On clouds that lift above the morning fog
That covers Trasimeno, the quattrocento
Bridge across a gorge, this road, this hill . . .

And I'm afraid I have been tricked again.
Not that the fresco is not beautiful,
But that I'm not looking at what's really here.
And this becomes another of the things
I can't come back to. What would I see?
Already I begin to notice men on horses,
A flock of sheep, two cows, the infant Christ.
Flaubert said art should set us dreaming.
Could he have meant it? Could he have meant
For me to miss the point completely?
To let Jesus and the Magi disappear?
And to find, instead, the deep-green beds of moss
I could see perfectly beneath the crystal
Waters of Clitumnus, just this morning,
Amazed that anything should be so clear.

The Presence of the Lute

after Vermeer's *Woman with a Wine Glass*

Next to me, a mother shows her child
The miracle, how you can see the glass
As well as the woman's face it covers.
The guide says, "The presence of the lute
Suggests something amorous." I had guessed,
Something eager in the cloaked man's stance,
His hand poised on the carafe to pour her more.
But, now, the lute's round bottom, jutting
From a chair, is ominous. The woman's glass
Trembles in her hands. She drinks too fast.
And everything else is known: how, soon,
She will not wear the fur-trimmed velvet jacket,
The salmon-colored skirt, that suddenly
Reveal their hidden purpose and intimate
The skin beneath. Arms, legs, thighs, breasts,
Vivid as the perfect silks and velvets.
Every item in the room at once conspires—
The sunlight, the tablecloth, the picture
On the wall all quiver like the lute's
Extended strings. And there is no returning
To the quiet, ordered room, its polished
Surfaces. I realize I have seen too much,
Not just this, but the lute in every picture,
Blurring every photograph of us,
Obscuring every outline, smearing colors,
Leaving each of us without a face,
Until only the lute itself is visible,
The curving wood, the bridge, the straining neck,
The four long white strings taut but motionless,
Stretched across the dark, expectant space.

Two

To an Unknown Russian Poet

for MB

Once, in a course on Russian literature,
The professor read a poem by a woman.
I did not catch her name but I remember
Something like "Louise," and a surname
Beginning with a "G" that must have ended
In "ova." He read in Russian and made up
His own translation as he went along.
There was a woman at an open window
And the color blue. She was longing
For something. I think a lover had left her,
But there was more than the lover, much more,
Something inexpressible in our language,
Needing thick, slurred vowels, heavy gutturals,
Sounds heard chanted in eerie churches
Crowded with icons, whose golden backgrounds
Shone and then receded into darkness
As the candles hung before them blinked in wind.

I can't even say what time of day it was,
But I imagine it was early evening,
Venus risen, but the sky still pale,
The lamps in her neighbors' doorways still unlit.
I'm sure it was autumn, that she looked across
The square at swaying birches, their gold leaves
Like the slender, ancient coins once strung
In necklaces for Persian dancers, and
Wound around their hips and breasts and arms
To move as they moved, and to make that low,

Metallic, sultry sound with every motion
That Louise began to hear as it grew dark.

She called it wind in trees and leaned far out
Of her open window, wanting to hear it.
She wrapped a thick, blue shawl around her shoulders
As the night grew cold. I will make it cashmere.
She had beautiful things. A Fabergé egg
With a tiny clock on it in diamonds,
A diary bound in kidskin and pure gold.
But what she wanted, what she wanted . . .

I think she stayed in that window for
The rest of her life. She came to know the movement
Of the light as something intimate,
Had private names for the changing colors.
The blue house on the square, for example,
She called "lupine" at noon in summer, at tea-time
In late November it became "dark pearl."
She knew when each of the two-tiered crosses
In her vista glinted in sunlight,
When each went dark against a darkened sky
And the square filled up with yellow rectangles
And globes. And if it was a moonless night,
Or cloudy, she'd wait up. She'd watch her neighbors'
Windows darken, one by one, and then,
In a single instant, all the streetlamps
Would carry with them everything she knew,
Square, birches, houses, crosses, everything.
And she would lean out her window, staring
At the blackness with a perfect calm,
Willing it to bring on her procession:
Drape after drape of rippling tapestry
With her lithe self on every one of them,

A cryptic, burning object in each hand
And an inscription hardly visible
Among the flowers woven in the background,
Written in her own, her perfect, hand.

January 1985

It is nothing less than a revelation,
A part of all this bitterness is beauty:
The cold, clear dazzle of reflecting snow
And not a cloud, the rivers motionless,
The sunlight tentative in just-bared woods.
Riding to see your brother, on the bus
To New Jersey, I could pick out two stripes,
One red, one blue, on an airplane flying
In the opposite direction. Some trick
Of motion canceling out motion made
It seem to hang mid-air, like something cut
From a magazine and pasted on
A vast, flat sky, only more frightening
Than that. The world was not itself.

The few left-over leaves didn't shiver.
I passed a pair of frozen-over ponds
And I envied them, stopped like that, on fire,
The airplane's giant wings glinting silver.
I was trying to realize that a living
Thing can die, that you had done that.
And it seemed the ponds had stopped in your honor,
The wind, the plane, all paralyzed for your sake.
And I couldn't do anything like that,
Could only look out the window at the spikes
Of ice and go on. I was going to fall
In love anyway, marry your brother,
And the rest of the frozen season,
Your threshold, your blinding carpet,
Was, for me, just biding time.

I was the only person on the street

On that exceptionally bitter night
That closed the shops and restaurants
And froze so many cars that they suspended
Alternate side of the street parking.
I walked along on pavements pocked with salt,
Each grating, railing, door, plastic trash bag
Cordoned off by a thin, dry edge of ice,
In air so clear it seemed to freeze the light
So that I saw, not by streetlamps, but by
Cold itself, the thin, white plumes of breath
That floated from my mouth and rose and curled
And held, like veils, beside my head.

Deceptions: Leah

All that time you
Worked for my sister,
I embroidered veils:
White, with gold threads
Running through.

They brought me one
Most gentle night, beneath
Smooth hands, while
The warm voice of Jacob
Whispered, "Rachel."

In winter England, I wanted to embroider Africa.
I visited the shops daily, choosing colors,
And ended up with every purple ever made,
Eleven greens and so much red and orange
I bought the same persimmon seven times.
Every day I concentrated: Africa.
There would be flowers large as people's heads,
Unimagined vegetables, shelves of toy-store animals,
Unstuffed and running wild, leaping over high,
Exotic grass, only known to flourish
In unnavigated depths of inmost Africa.

I found a good-sized remnant of velvet,
Jet-black, gleaming like a jaguar's skin,
And christened Africa with chartreuse thread
Which sprouted almost instantly to vines,
To ferns, to unfamiliar leaves and stems,
Offering ginger and antheriums
In almost no time. I was cultivating orchids
When I suddenly remembered Madagascar
And went running to the store for blue,
Deliberating several hours what shade
Would be profound enough to manifest
The deepest of all oceans.

By vernal equinox the Eastern Coast was done,
Each beach composed entirely of ground-up jewels
Fallen from a nearby precious mountain.
There would be peaks of topaz, blue diamond
And in the distance a volcanic burst
So dazzling the natives would believe

A thousand years of prophecy fulfilled,
Their savior on a giant, ivory stag
With great, pearl wings about to come.

Oh Africa, I stayed with you while England
Wrestled with spring like some swindler
Demanding blessings from an angel.
I tended mangoes through the whole ordeal
Of crocuses. The days slowly widened
Like expectant moons, what with the skies
Spreading themselves out, smoothing their edges,
Preparing for the stars like tablecloths
Waiting for their knives and forks and spoons.
Often I would fall asleep by daylight,
Waterfalls cascading into tangles
On my lap as I dreamed of working
Cockatoos with outstretched wings.

I was trying out a tiger when the roses
Parachuted into England. Those secretive
Blossoms covered everything, with more
Finality, more grace, even, than snow.
Whole cathedrals disappeared, highways
Vanished. Every village on the island
Was vermillion or scarlet or the color
That the French call, simply, "rose."

How could I have overlooked defense?
Not a single tribesman, not one lion
And seven thousand roses scaling
My stone walls, aiming at the very heart
Of Central Africa. A lone gazelle
Scuttled to the nearest palm as plains,
Jungles, beaches, all of Africa—
Ablaze with half a tiger and my prize

Giraffe, with perfect spots and one moist eye—
Was folded up with all the other continents,
Without Kilimanjaro or even a cloud
To designate her distant sky.

After Midnight, the Fifth Month

I am becoming a cathedral! My
Belly rises from the bed like a tiny
Model of the Florence *Cupolone*.
Probably a belly just like this
Inspired Brunelleschi's great design:
The original, the perfect, home.
There is a tapping from the inside,
Gentle, almost imperceptible,
Like piano hammers touching piano strings.
And I am fluent in these first attempts
At language; I am turned to someone else.
There *is* life beyond our own. Gabriel
Whispers, softly fluttering his wings,
With every touch a hushed annunciation.

Five A.M., *the Ninth Month*

Your kick awakens me to wild geese
Honking overhead, the stirring trees
Just visible beneath the new, pale blue.
Everything is coming: day, spring, you;
The geese above all seem to shout, "Make way!"
But I would almost keep you where you are,
Your pulse at breakneck speed turning the air
I breathe into a future, wind on clay,
Your heart galloping beneath my heart
And every living thing I hear, its echo,
Geese and wind in trees and my own heart,
The whole unwakened world resounds with you,
Shaking until life itself will part
And you—imagine—you'll come screaming through.

Nadezhda Learns of the Poet's Death

We shall sit together in the kitchen for a while. . . .
Sharp knife, a loaf of bread . . .
So we can leave here for the station
Where we must hope no one will find us out.
                    —OSIP MANDELSTAM, 1931

She has lived for years
In preparation, his words pressed
In the tough fist
Of her heart.

She checks once more
For each wild bee, every swallow,
And clenches them tightly
With ice and star,
The knife and bread
Upon her table,

Ready to depart, without him,
For the station.

From the train, she scans
The fleeting landscape, now
Expressionless with snow.
She whispers a poem and his voice,
Unforgettable, rises to escort her
To the border.

Three

Babel

Think of the evolution of sand to glass.
From all this grinding down, there may yet come
A clarity, as if living were a language
You get to know just by being in a place.
I hold on to this hope with reverence
For the miracle of ancient, fragile goblets
Dug up whole, the visions in medieval windows.
Is it clarity or obfuscation? You can
Never tell with things like God or love
And no amount of pummeling will ever
Keep you from believing. There is a certain
Dinginess to knowledge, as if the world
Got stuck in its rotation at the end
Of autumn. No matter what we learn we love.

But for a while, after a particularly
Brutal lesson, you live through a period
Of getting errands done, appliances repaired,
Letters answered, lightbulbs in the ceiling switched.
The smell of pressed linen lingers in the kitchen.
But on the moment of return from the picture
Framers, when you stop to catch your breath
Before searching out the hammer and nails,
You cannot avoid what you have worked
So hard to avoid. There is no metaphor
For this; you have to call it pain.

Instead, on the telephone, you call it bravery.
You don't mean to be condescending.
But, what I am, if you want to know,

Is foolish, talking like this, when you
Won't even own up to speaking the language.

Surely, the most awful punishment was Babel.
To know that what you say is meaningless.
No wonder they fell from such a height.
I know the tower was probably made of granite,
But I hear its destruction as the shattering of glass,
Can see the shards catch their glints of sun and scatter.
Who would dare to build with such a history?
And passion, in any case, is so peculiar a language.

I have heard of children forgetting the language
They were reared in. The unused words dangle
At the back of the mind and gradually fall.
They are said to return in dreams, but no one
Knows this. I have only seen them disappear,
Utterly, without a word of memory or warning.

Letter from Florence

Most nights I dream the same dream: letters.
I hear the postman's car stop, and him, unknowing,
Leaving his engine on, the thump
Of paper hitting paper as the letters fall,
The engine turning over. . . .
I study postmarks, return addresses, stamps.
Most vivid is a pair of painted fans from China.

But the other night, I dreamed one of those
Dreams you're embarrassed to tell about:
A high, distant place I thought was Srinagar,
In Kashmir. Cascades. A turquoise pool.
Such clear water you could see the future in it.
There were men swimming all around me.
I looked for you. I can't remember too much else;
I confuse it with a stamp from the other dream.
The turquoise color, the height of the place,
Pellucid water with the sunlight making patterns
Like a tarot deck, the woman on the stake,
The thick, black blindfold, the buzzards,
The panic, the ache, the looking for you.

A couple of days ago your letter came,
A gray stamp with a profile of the Queen.
You are not sleeping well, have money problems,
Dream of opening a bookshop in Dalston Junction.
I'm not sleeping badly. I'm always tired
From the long walk, uphill, home.

It's dark as ever once the streetlights end,
Especially on nights when there's no moon.

(In my dream, I never open letters.
Such fine, white envelopes, ivory, ecru,
I watch them pile up like snow.)

Didn't you walk up with me once, or was that
Another dream? A car passed by and blinded us.
We stopped, waiting for the heavy black
To make itself a row of cypresses,
The thick gray shades to reappear. Finally,
The stars emerged, trailing yellow stripes
And sky began to separate from cypresses,
To leave between each pair of trees a long, gray blade
Until the whole sky was hung with knives.

International Call

Silence on the telephone is always difficult,
But on long distance calls it has the added
Resonance of money piling up, the scenery
Your voice must cross to reach the other side,
Views from outer space, since they started
Using satellite communications. What I mean
Is the irrevocable sound of failure.

When you speak, it's to divide yourself,
What this part wants, what that part wants.
I am remembering the day you left
Your heart open accidentally, how I
Looked in and saw what Saint Augustine says
That God sees when He looks at the world:
No past, no future, but the whole story
Of the universe simultaneous, present,
From the time He pulled the water out of dry land.

I want to tell you things, to say we are not doomed
To repeat the disasters of the world, or your
Old disasters, that a person who has loved badly
Can love well. This is a universe of constant changes.

But I'm beginning to think that there is pain
At the center of everything, like the lava
They taught about in school at the center
Of the world, the layers of the earth's crust
Always vulnerable and each change like
A separate season of the elements,
Unrepeatable. Wood. Coal. Diamond.

So many millions of years to achieve

That hardness, and still danger of returning
To the unformed void at any time.
A jolt might do it, a fault in the surface,
Or some stray foreign matter, a meteorite
Or even just a sound from outer space,
Your disembodied voice, now fortified
By distance, like the penny they also
Taught about, falling from a high place,
That would shatter anything in its path.

Four

A Poem About Angels

You want to write a poem about angels.
Not because they are winged and white and haloed
And in many paintings very beautiful
But because you have seen many things and remembered
Only angels. You are certain, for example,
That you walked on famous streets,
Under towers, over rivers, around the parapets
Of ancient walls, medieval walls.

Once, you watched beeches turn to cypress
From a moving train, and every time you looked,
Another season. Surely there were mountains
By the side of the road. You wrote it down.

Only the angels are intact, marble
Or otherwise, recorded, you imagine, before breakfast,
Maybe before dawn, by some lucky visionary
With a paintbrush. You believed especially
The story of the man who fell asleep and woke
To find his Mary finished by the angels.
You would like to know those thorough angels
With names like Gabriel, the cherubim, the seraphim.

All you know is how impossible it is
Without them. The stones conspire against you
With the heavy clouds, and everything through glass
Or, worse, that cracking memory, flashing tents
And camels in between the high pink towns
Of, was it Tuscany, as if the slides you never took

Got all mixed up. Only occasional the empty screen
For you to fill with all your angels.

In the dim church, a darker patch of wall,
The handiwork of angels. A face
More gentle than the finished circle
Of a moon altering your courtyard,
Unhinging buildings from their heavy stones.

The angels could help you with anything.
They could show you how to use a word like *dream*
Or *I* in the middle of a poem, pressing you
With secrets like their oldest friends,
Prophets, patriarchs, and kings.

Still, they're busy with gardening
And God to deal with who is old
And must be disappointed. I suppose
The scenery gets dull, if you're
An angel. All that cloud and pearl.
There aren't chariots of fire
Every day, you know, and it's a long time
Between appearances in dreams.

One night, they are gathered on a cloud.
A moon, completed, rises, catches them off guard
And before they think that is another month
And I have done nothing, one cries, "Gabriel,
Look, Gabriel." And Gabriel, transformed,
Puts down his harp, which he has been playing
Only mechanically for the last two weeks,
And hums a long-dreamed psalm.

The Yiddish Muses

I—unneeded, a poet among Jews—
Growing, like wild grass, from a soil not ours. . . .
In an alien world I sing of the cares
Of men in a desert beneath alien stars.
                              —MANI LEIB (1883–1953)

They arrive, always, unexpected,
Silent as the glide of angels
On six wings. Only the idea of sound,
Wind that for a moment might be ocean.
I want to catch them, to make something
For them, a city or at least a psalm,
But I have nothing to build it with.
Yiddish is no language for poetry, so homely
On the page, vowels instead of silences.

Unneeded, a poet among Jews,
I end up wandering the streets
With unknown visitors, who speak
In a language round and thick
As pillows squashed against my head.
They are telling dreams, so old,
So corny, dreamed by now in almost
Every language and a few elements:
Wood, stone, even gold, preserved
In cloth with needles and silk thread.

They have left a little dreaming
Everywhere: watery cities, towered cities,
Even in Córdoba, blank with sun, so white
And so unlikely, they left a whole room
Engraved with psalms. Judah Halevi

Left a palace and a family. Tired
Of poetry and dreams, he headed East.
After that, no one is certain.
They say he was trampled by a Turkish horse
As he kissed the earth, arriving in Jerusalem.

You will tell me this is not a pleasant story,
But you know nothing about dreams.
What would have happened if the sun
Had bowed to Joseph? I know for a fact
It would have killed him and any unsuspecting
Bystanders. I suppose we must be patient
Here, at the stony end of the ladder.
Only angels can go up and come back down.

I stay awake nights, though I'd give
Anything to see the curved backs
Of stars, and wonder who needs ladders
With three sets of wings. I watch shadows,
Cast by my Venetian blinds, stretch
Across the ceiling like the tracks
For unknown trains. Can you blame me
If I ride and ride, unneeded as I am
And dangerous, a dreamer among Jews?

The muses burst out laughing, "Some dream."
All morning, in synagogue, they chuckle
As they praise The Name, "Some prize to be a traveler
Among Jews." Still, they manage silence
For the eighteen prayers, establishing that routine
Miracle, reordering of heavens, Jerusalem
Rising like the sun above their heads,
Above, even, the women's section, higher
Than any memory its walls and domes.

Looking for Angels in New York

All this traveling around and I've learned
Nothing less obvious than this: that each
Piece of the world has something missing.
Home again, I have forgotten the stops of the trains,
My friends' phone numbers. I haven't even the heart
To take the maps out, to say, "Here I have been,
Here and here." I want to explain that there
Can be no adequate descriptions, but you will think
I mean the differences are insurmountable,
When it is this vast sameness over everything
I cannot name, the thing you wait for
And do not believe in when it's come and gone,
The words that will not stand still
Long enough for you to take a picture.

My friend asks questions and I answer.
He says he read the Metropolitan Life
Building is based on something Italian.
I look at it and shrug. "Not that I know,"
And then I see the campanile of San Marco,
Squat, granite, white instead of red.
It will become my personal comfort
In the skyline, one of those public things
You have no right to but you say you own.

If Jacob had rested in New York, he
Would have seen angels on elevators,
And Saint Mark, though an insurance salesman,
Would certainly have witnessed miracles.

I don't necessarily have to see
An angel, I just want to see some wings,

Even a flash of them, gliding, moving
Up and out, a balloon some child
Has let go of, smaller and smaller in
The sky, only wings, definite, white wings.

From the number seven train out to Queens,
A chance glimpse of the Unisphere brings
The future in its purest form, the whole
World connected by picture telephones
And cars that look like earthbound rocketships.
Odd that they should have left the silver globe
Still standing there, now the children it was
Built for have all grown. The space between the
Continents seems eerie now, foreboding,
And the dazzling modern sculpture weirdly
Archaic, almost shocking, like the face
Of a great movie star no longer young.

Who would have thought that people would reject
The picture telephone, the moving sidewalk,
That I would come home from all my travels
To New Jersey, to settle for a bit
Of quiet and some green, and the moment
On the hill before the Lincoln Tunnel
When I really do possess something extraordinary.
Loyal, I pick out my Metropolitan Life,
At night drenched in a white light almost blue.
Who can know that by day it is not brick
And red and surrounded by a great piazza
Opening on water, that, in the huge
White space we cannot see, there is no thick
Flock of cooing pigeons, taking off, alighting,
In a constant, dreamy fluttering of wings.

Dawn

God must know He's being ostentatious.
And yet He worked so hard at His distinctions,
Dark from light, night from day, He can't
Just push the stars smoothly on their way
And watch the colors ease from black to blue.
Must He restrain Himself? Or may He show,
For one brief instant, some of His secrets,
How He can pull a moment outside time,
Streak the sky. He must miss those six good days.

So there's a moment every morning
The sleepless can rely on, the night-shift
Workers, the revelers, the people
Whom the day has failed. New York City's towers
Seem almost natural. I sometimes think
I see them wipe their eyes, blinking east
As, dazed, they lift their heads up from the gray.
Dawn, even from a midtown skyscraper,
Is beautiful. Cement and glass, as if
Still dreaming, tentative. The long, lazy
Stretch of yawning stone. The line of buildings
On the park is suddenly a pale hedge of lilacs.
Who am I to say it is no dream?

Who, with all this glory in front of me,
See only myself clearly, find myself
In the changing oranges, the purple-reds.
What am I weeping for? I could also
Disappear in the city that I thought
I knew, go where the violet goes, instead
Of waiting for the buildings to emerge

As they always do, and resolidify,
Before I've had a chance really to see.
For in this minute, surely, is the opportunity:
God carried away, His defenses down,
The very shape of the window altered,
And whoever does the talking whispering,
"Possible," in a voice that would be wind
If this were the world where there are winds.

It is not that world. It is not a light trick,
Either. But there's no holding it;
You have to move, not dawdle in a haze
Of pink, remembering your six, good days.
The colors dissipate, the fire rises
And everything returns intact, to dare
You to believe what you have seen. The sun
Is yellow now. And I have missed again
That last split second of transition.
I suppose it's purely His. Call it nostalgia.
Or perhaps He really recreates the world
As the legend says, heaven, earth,
The sun, the moon, the fish, the animals,
A city crowded with the namers of names,
Who will awaken shortly, unaware
Of any miracle, while we, who have
Very nearly seen, go back to work
Or to our beds, hoping we can try again.
Perhaps we only blinked our eyes, turned
Our heads. Perhaps it wasn't beyond us.

Questions, After York Minster
Was Struck by Lightning

Who ever heard of a cathedral struck by lightning?
I am inclined to make a bad joke, to say
God was after the insurance money,
And then make out a check for the restoration.
But I can't shake the notion—call it superstition—
That this is a clear sign. The wrath of God.
Or His broken heart. Or His frustration.
Sadly, we can never know the details,
Only the fierceness of it, the evidence:
The black rose window, the ruined ceiling,
The charred, uncovered space where I once thought
I saw the infinite encompassed.
Even in a blurry photograph
It seems to echo with the prophet's voice:
"I will not hear: your hands are full of blood."

Cromwell might point to this as vindication
Of his trips around the country smashing glass,
As if God were finishing at last the work he started.
And a Jew, with his memory for massacres,
Might bring up Clifford's Tower, eleven-ninety,
And say York has no business with a house of God.
Eleven-ninety to nineteen-eighty-four
Was nothing to Him. He took a nap first.
(Which would certainly explain a lot of things.)
Perhaps He had a bad dream; He saw
The whole extravaganza in His sleep:
The moors, the lightning, the cathedral

And here on earth it happened. Just like that.
Who does the interpretations when God dreams?

A psychiatrist would call it self-destruction.
I have a friend who rips up pictures
Of herself, favorite possessions, letters.
She won't have people looking at them
When she's dead. She's melodramatic.
But then, by all accounts of things, so is God.
So was Michelangelo, throwing
A chisel at his final *Pietà,*
The one in which he used his face for God
The Father's. He said He didn't get Christ's
Torso right. He hated the contorted arm
And Moses smashed his tablets on the ground.
Imagine the tedium of piecing
The commandments back together, shard by shard.
I've often wondered if he regretted it,
If my friend regrets her lost mementos.
I have seen the cracks in Christ's contorted arm,
The stony face of the Magdalene
Another sculptor had to finish.
It's hard to think that lightning was an accident.

There is the issue of the English Reformation.
Four hundred fifty years ago, *exactly,*
When the king was desperate to marry Anne Boleyn,
His great cathedrals ceased to look to Rome.
And Henry the Eighth's lineage: the House
Of York. For some this would be proof enough,
Saint Peter reinforced by lightning
And the righteous Thomas More at last avenged.

But in the places where the sun once never set,
They might see in this a different

Retribution, a rare coalition:
Osiris, Krishna, Allah, Buddha, Shiva
And all the other gods and prophets
And heavenly warriors slighted by
The missionaries' singsong hymns, the pink
They spread across the map, the certainty.

Or perhaps God's aim is failing after all
These years. He was trying for a missile base.
(Can a missile be struck by lightning?
This seems to me my most worthwhile question.)
Or perhaps He was aiming for another
Country altogether. This is the problem
With an act of God. Who explains it?
No prophet. No writing on the walls.
I suppose He saw the uselessness of explanations.
In our hands, even God's words are ambiguous,
The way we are inclined to give words wings,
Interpreting and reinterpreting
Until the very word *meaning* eludes us,
Like some untranslatable nuance
From another language, something essential,
That we can just pretend to understand.

It's true that history repeats itself.
Just look at us, back again at Babel:
A great stone edifice to heaven ruined
And language flying off in a thousand
Directions, absolutely aimless,
Offering no help to us at all.

Because the truth is the reasons are innumerable.
We have not done well with our world.
Of course, a bolt of lightning can't change that,
But God has tied His hands, He's made promises.

It's no good creating in your own image;
Things turn out unexpectedly grotesque.

So the Minster is struck by lightning.
Perhaps He won't have people looking at it
When He's dead. Or maybe He hopes still
That we will see that gutted cathedral
And something will happen. The very day
After the fire it was full of people.
Surely some of them had come to pray.

He was probably only half listening.
The other half was dreaming up His next
Creation, covering His mirrors, thinking
Next time only He would name the names,
When a boy soprano caught his attention,
Singing a new setting to a psalm.
And the voice was as pure as His favorite,
David's, language, about the beauty
Of the world that God had made. And He
Was the God the boy was singing about.
He had designed those mountains, those cedars,
The voice that praised His Name. He couldn't help it;
In spite of everything, He was proud
Of the music He had singlehandedly
Invented. Had He imagined quite this sound
When He fashioned all those tiny strings?
Or did He hear it echoing through endless
Vaults and arches, filling up a vast,
High, covered space and held there, resonant,
Beneath a final vault of wood and stone,
Like the one they could rebuild, in time, below.

Five

To Eva

Born: D.P. camp, Lanzburg, Germany, March 21, 1947
Died: New Jersey, January 9, 1985

As usual, the seasons change too fast.
This year's early balmy spell so leisurely,
Convincing, it tricks even the cautious
White magnolia into opening
And giving up its petals to a sudden
Change of air, to scatter on the ground
Like a thousand schoolgirl hopes to pluck, "he loves me."
Forsythia and crocus, from a distance,
Are confetti, what crowds in Venice
Throw into the air at *Carnivale*
To color streets for two weeks into Lent.
That's what the willow branches look like,
Even close up, or some oriental
Decoration for the year of the dragon,
Dripping long, chartreuse crepe-paper scales.
And I would so much rather be waking
To a sky like the inside of a shell,
The nearly invisible gray-white chambers,
Swirl enfolding swirl in clouds of snow,
Establishing a clear, white, soundless
Distance between place and place, all pale
Until the twisted stretch of branches starts
To darken over bars of rose and gold,
Looking like that kindergarten trick
Of covering a wildly crayoned picture
With a heavy coat of black, then scratching back
The colors with a pin. And I would watch
Those leafless trees even without a sunset,
All those previously well-kept secrets
In the open air, wayward arrows,

Umbrella frames turned inside out in wind.
Commuting, through the thinnest gauze of snow,
I would watch them from the window, knowing what
The world will look like when there is no world,
How its ghosts will haunt the empty space.

And what happened to you was almost
Tolerable on those days. At least
It didn't screech the way it screeches now
Against these garish blossoms floating lies
Up and down the Northeast Corridor,
Until even I am starting to believe them,
Smelling lilac, grabbing crimson beds
Of tulips with the corner of my eye,
Mauve azaleas. For your father, it must
Be like his first, lurid days out of Dachau,
Europe a bizarre, trick continent,
The same names on the signposts of the towns,
On the railway platforms, on the street signs,
The same shops, the same houses, the same doors,
And the people, if anything at all,
Hallucinations. It was spring then, too,
Not that he noticed it, though I would bet
He knew the season two springs later. You
Were the rarest of the rare, a person *born*.
The others must have envied your grandmother
When she got you to fill her empty name.
Now it's back again, with all those hundreds
And hundreds of thousands of unused extras,
In a vast invisible pile, like those
Famous piles of eyeglasses and shoes,
Waiting for the Messiah, I guess,
When the bodies of the dead will rise,
Asking questions of the rabbis among them.
Does the prophecy include the decomposed,
The graveless? Will they come alive as soap

And parchment and blankets or their old selves?
What will happen if the soap's been used,
The parchment printed on? The talmudists
Will work it out in singsong arguments,
Gesturing at blackboards made of air.

What they decide will not apply to you.
You died in better times, you had a service,
A grave, a tombstone, prayers for the dead.
Even the seasons cooperated,
Though, of course, they resumed their schedule
In no time, almost as oblivious
As the railway lines that still persist
In pushing Europe eastward, making stops
That shouldn't exist, bringing mail to them.
You would have thought that they would change the names,
That the earth would turn to salt, or something,
That this spring would at least have declared
Some brief moratorium, not come
So early, at least, so sure of itself,
Dragging cherry blossoms streaked with rain.
Look at them, an Impressionist might have
Painted them. See how they expose
Those frauds for what they were, opportunists,
Taking advantage of a freakish storm
To paint the world as petals smeared with rain,
As if they'd made it up, a new art form
Out of this horrible freak of nature
They catch before the real catastrophe
When everything comes down in heavy wind
And the shaken trees, lost, just stand there,
Thinking this isn't supposed to happen,
Isn't the order of things, unlearning
Everything they know, while, all around,
The spring regains composure, flourishes,
And at their feet the petals mimic snow.

The Contemporary Poetry Series

Edited by Paul Zimmer